# Work *That* Works
# Work *That* Wins

Marcio Moreira

# Work *That* Works
# Work *That* Wins

authorHOUSE®

*AuthorHouse™*
*1663 Liberty Drive*
*Bloomington, IN 47403*
*www.authorhouse.com*
*Phone: 833-262-8899*

*Cover photo ©Mark Schäfer*
*Back cover photo ©Joaquim Pedro Martins Moreira*

*Published by AuthorHouse   07/17/2020*

*ISBN: 978-1-7283-5935-9 (hc)*
*ISBN: 978-1-7283-5934-2 (e)*

*Library of Congress Control Number: 2020906955*

*Print information available on the last page.*

*This book is printed on acid-free paper.*

This book is dedicated to the memory of
Marcio Martins Moreira

1947—2014

# Table Of Contents

# Acknowledgements

## "The Boy From Brazil"

For many years Marcio, "the boy from Brazil", worked at McCann Worldgroup. His first real job was a projectionist at McCann Erickson in São Paulo, at the age 19. He then stayed in one agency for 44 years, retiring in November of 2011.

In his own, unique way, he was a man of the world, a family man, a role model and a mentor who touched and personally guided careers and lives of many people. He was a great believer in new blood, new craftsmanship, new energy, new leadership and fresh ideas. Marcio was also a voracious reader, spoke fluently several languages (even made an attempt to speak Mandarin) and an extremely skilled raconteur.

"Work *That* Works, Work *That* Wins" is a compilation of some of Moreira's admirable and valuable collection of lectures throughout the world at universities and industry forums.

Marcio devoted the bulk of his professional career to the creative end of the business and most of the results he was associated with must be shared with other team players.

By publishing this book I celebrate the life and work of a man who carries a memorable legacy; of leadership, creativity and service that will be talked about for many years to come and will serve as inspiration to many and future generations.

On behalf of Marcio, a special thanks to Tom Hackett and Washington Olivetto for their compassion, generosity and kindness in helping putting this book together; to Sarah Bass, Diane Merklinger, John Dooner, Peter Hamilton, Bob James, Percival Caropreso, and to all his McCann Team around the world, to everyone, colleagues and friends, for your professional and invaluable friendship. Forgive me if some have not been mentioned, but know that your contribution is appreciated. And now it is time to give back.

*—Maria A. Moreira*

Marcio Moreira ©Mark Schäfer

## **Marcio Moreira** *The Renaissance Man...*

That's what many called Marcio. Whether creating cook books, classic jazz, whether delivering a virtuoso performance or being a patient teacher. Marcio was our guru for all things creative.

"Work *That* Works, Work *That* Wins" includes a collection of his talks on a subject Marcio knew best— ***Creativity***.

*—John J. Dooner*
*Chairman Emeritus McCann Worldgroup*

Washington Olivetto ©Marcelo Tabach

# Introduction

## More Alive Than Ever

Marcio Moreira was the most international of all advertising professionals.

He was able to be an American in New York, a Venezuelan in Caracas, Japanese in Tokyo, a Turk in Istanbul and an Argentinian in Buenos Aires, without ever ceasing to be a Brazilian.

With the actor's talent developed in his youth, a lifetime passion for songwriting and his natural born skill as a salesman, Marcio Moreira was a complete and globalized advertising man, even before the globalization concept was coined.

There was a time when ad agencies were divided between those who claimed to be *effective* and those who claimed to be *creative*—the money-makers and the award-winners. Something like right-wing and left-wing parties in politics. The efficient ones were the right-wing and the creative were the left-wing.

The agencies owned by large corporate groups such as McCann, J. Walter Thompson and Young & Rubican were right-wing.

The independent agencies such as Chiat Day, Abbot Mead & Vickers and DPZ were left-wing.

As a result of this pseudo-ideological clash, people from the large groups and independent agencies were almost never seen together. The only exception was Marcio. He knew how to mix on both sides.

I met Marcio Moreira in the early 70's when he was creative leader of McCann-Brazil, at the time the largest agency in the country and also considered dull and right-wing. I was the brightest star at DPZ, the 6th largest agency and also the coolest and seen as left-wing.

Obviously, this right-wing/left-wing stuff was nonsense in an industry which understood that the best thing about capitalism was to be capitalist. However, we were living in a country when a military dictatorial government ruled.

So it was automatically assumed that Marcio and I would be enemies. But as soon as we met, we became friends—and loved each other. So much so that years later I was the bearer of an offer from Ed McCabe, for Marcio and I to be partners in a New York independent agency—a left-wing agency. And Marcio was McCann's bearer of an invitation to join him at the New York Office—a right-wing agency.

Neither of which happened. We went on with our lives but continued to be very close. And when I had the idea of blending right-wing and left-wing by merging my agency W/Brasil with McCann, it was Marcio who made it happen. That's how WMcCann was born.

When Marcio decided to retire he told me personally and the idea was hatched of having his farewell party in Cap D'Antibes, because there in the South of France was where the biggest and most diverse names and talents in the world of advertising mingled. A fitting place for a giant of the industry to celebrate his career.

This book can only capture some of what made Marcio so special. He leaves us here some of his thoughts, insights and predictions for the industry he loved. What he left for friends like me is *saudades*, a word for a kind of melancholy and sadness that only exists in Portuguese a language in which Marcio was truly a poet. But despite my *saudades* I have the memories of our times together, and those memories will always bring him back to me.

*—Washington Olivetto*
*Founder of W/Brasil and WMcCann*

# Biography
## 1947-2014

Marcio M. Moreira was born in São Paulo, Brazil in 1947. He was just 19 years old when he started working for McCann-Erickson Brazil as a projectionist. By the time he retired in 2011 he was not only instrumental in some famous Coca-Cola ads of all times, he had risen to be Vice-Chairman, Chief Creative Officer of the world's largest global agency network and simultaneously Asia-Pacific Regional Director before going on to become the group's Chief Talent Officer and Worldwide HR Director. No challenge was too much, no responsibility too big and there was no doubt in his mind about the global power of creativity.

The young Brazilian projectionist had been at the São Paulo office for just a couple of years before he was made Associate Creative Director and in 1971 was dispatched as writer/producer to work in London, Lisbon, Copenhagen and Frankfurt.

He returned to Brazil in 1974, becoming Creative Director of McCann-Erickson Brazil and subsequently Creative Director for all of South America.

He was constantly commuting to New York and Atlanta working

on Coca-Cola and in 1980 Marcio was asked to come to New York full time to lead McCann-Erickson's elite InterNational Team, the agency's specialized creative task force that worked for major multi-national clients including Coca-Cola and which operated out of London, New York and Hong Kong.

In 1984 he became the International Creative Director for Mc-Cann-Erickson Worldwide. Then in 1987 Marcio took a one year leave of absence to work as Worldwide Marketing Coordinator for Columbia Pictures in Hollywood California, the studio then being a Coca-Cola subsidiary.

On his return he continued in his role with the InterNational Team. In 1990 he became an American Citizen and in 1991 became Vice-Chairman and Chief Creative Officer International and from 1991-1994 this also included responsibilities for the New York office's creative department.

In 1994 Marcio also took on the job of Regional Director for Mc-Cann Asia-Pacific, the region's largest western-based advertising agency system spanning over 20 countries, $1.7 billion in billing and employing over 2500 people.

In 1999 he was not only Vice-Chairman, Chief Creative Officer but also Director of Global Brand Management.

From 2003 to his retirement in 2011 Marcio was Vice-Chairman, Chief Talent Officer and Worldwide HR Director.

Marcio had come a long way from the projection booth. And retirement didn't slow him down. He continued to teach, judge and inspire. He was a board member of VCU Adcenter and The Berlin School of Creative Leadership.

He was also a long-time member of the Brazilian-American

Chamber of Commerce and a big supporter of Brazilian culture and art.

During his career he had chaired and judged for advertising festivals all around the world.

Marcio was the recipient of scores of awards, winning all shades of Cannes Lions, Clios, Mobius and Andy Awards.

He was Brazil's Advertising Professional of the Year (1988) and the decade (1990) and of the century (2003).

He was a Clio Jury Member, a Judge and Chairman of the Cannes Festival and was the only person in the history of Cannes to have judged on behalf of two countries, Brazil and the United States. And in 1989 was President of the Jury. Marcio was also Chairman of the Board of Judges of the New York Festivals.

He was recipient of The Paul Foley Award, the highest creative honor bestowed by the Interpublic Group of Companies.

Marcio was also the architect of McCann Worldgroup's Human Futures Development education program for mid-level and senior executives in all the group's companies.

Marcio was fluent in Portuguese, Spanish, English and French. He was the author of two books, one a collection of poetry, the other a series of short stories. He co-authored the Brazilian edition of Richard Edler's book on leadership, *"If Only I Knew"*.

He was a recorded lyricist, having collaborated with leading jazz and bossa-nova artists such as Sadao Watanabe in Japan and Cesar Camargo Mariano in Brazil.

Marcio's multi-cultural expertise attracted the attention of Secretary of State Colin Powell and his Under-Secretary Charlotte Beers who recruited Marcio for a special communications program in the aftermath of the September 11 attacks. The project helped diffuse fear and distress of the US among Muslim communities at home and overseas.

Marcio was a talented manager of people. It was his fundamental skill. He understood the passions of creatives, the desires and needs of account managers in all the regions of the world. He was a natural born leader and relationship builder as well as a strong strategic thinker with an unrelenting creative spirit. The most iconic Coca-Cola campaigns of all time have his influence stamped all over them.

And from Goodyear to Unilever, Nestlé to Exxon/Esso and General Motors to UPS he helped shape the future of borderless creativity.

Marcio Moreira ©Mark Schäfer

*"Culture isn't defined by borders or language, anymore, it is defined by mindset, feelings and context."*

We live in the Age of Supply.

As the number of choices grew, customers became more demanding, more discriminating. What used to be a seller's market evolved into a buyer's market.

Advertising matured from a spontaneous form of persuasion into more precisely designed information. Consumer research became more of a science; advertising, less of an art form. This is the drawing of the Age of Demand. The views, attitudes and biases of consumers gained untold influence over the content and quality of marketing communications. Questions were asked, answers were given, results were tabulated, and road-maps were prepared for the creative process to follow.

Most often, this process produced effective advertising. As its best, it produced reliable work: advertising that promoted brands, sold products—even won awards!

Only infrequently did this process produce breakthrough communications that altered perceptions, expanded markets and helped brands transcend the products they represented.

In this brave new world—*Insight* is king.

*Insight Interpretation*, the key to the Kingdom.

To interpret a consumer insight is to use one's imagination—to take a calculated risk—to make the leap between knowing and projecting probable consumer behavior. It is to turn strategic planning into Stage One in the creative process. It is to turn insight interpreters into creative people themselves. Consumers do not read research reports. Consumers meet the message where the message happens: the screen, the page, the poster, the website, the t-shirt, the morning radio program.

Messages only mean something if they add to what consumers already know and feel. Windows, not mirrors. That's what messages should feel like to consumers. Possibilities, not reflections. That's what will impel them into action.

*"Create, not replicate.*
*See the world through fresh eyes.*
*Stand in a different place and describe what you see.*
*Speak with an original voice.*
*Connect what others have not seen as a connection.*
*Create messages that consumers wish to consume.*
*Dramatize a penetrating truth about your client's brands.*
*Tell the truth so well that the customer is converted."*

*"In this world two people will rule: the person with imagination and the person with the remote control."*

# Expanding Our Definition
# Of Creativity

Advertising's very currency is creativity. I believe creativity is a universal gift, which we may or may not choose to exercise. Most people, whether they work with creativity or not, are creative, in some way. This creativity can be expressed in the way they cook, the way they make love, the way they decorate their homes, the way they dress. When creativity is central to one's occupation—architecture, music, industrial design, literature, painting, sculpture, advertising, film-making—then it tends to be more visible, more palpable. Creative people share certain lifestyle traits such as a similar language, an attitude towards daily living, an approach to tasks at hand—that are recognizable. But creativity is not the exclusive province of those who use it professionally.

Paradoxically, creatives have been slavishly dependent on prevailing views of creativity. And although they design the work, they default to others to creatively judge it. Festivals, award shows, the trade press and the buzz on the street: this is what provides the framework of their creative self-worth. They know the rules of the game and they will continue to compete. After all, victory is sweet and fame is an aphrodisiac. Games are won by ingredients such as talent, style, stamina and perseverance.

Can creativity exist without talent, style, stamina, perseverance? I don't think so. In the artistic world, people like Beethoven, Picasso and Hemingway had to apply a considerable amount of all those things to achieve the greatness we now attribute to them. In advertising, a commercial form of creativity, the rigors are different (demanding clients; challenging strategies; interpreting consumer insights) but creativity only shines if talented people persevere through it all—without a loss in style!

This is a time of trouble for conventional creativity. There are few certainties left. It is a time of blur, a time of maybes. You unfold the map and it is blank. Or it contains imprecise, incomplete directions. Inhabiting a world controlled by others, creatives find themselves left to their own devices. Most of them were raised in a world characterized by "yeps" and "nopes", and now reside in a world of "ya knows", "likes" and "whatevers". They were moved from a neighborhood of oversimplification to Optionsville and the instructions manual to our navigational system has been misplaced. We have been put in Cyberage's witness relocation program.

My view is that creativity is about inventing things or combining things in a fresh way. Therefore, all that surrounds us counts: popular culture (music, fashion, design, styles); and technology definitely has enormous impact (from the written word to images on celluloid to the digital era in a few centuries.)

One of the biggest challenges is to sell exciting, innovative creative solutions. There's great uncertainty in the world, the mood is not for risk-taking and that seems to be true locally and globally. On the positive side, creativity is now an all-pervasive human manifestation, with many common traits, which makes it more universal, less parochial or provincial.

There was a time when all thought humor and music wouldn't travel—they were local in nature. Well, humor and music are two of the most powerful connectors in the world today—and it doesn't really matter where they come from!

In my experience, consumers are critical of things that are arrogant, annoying, boring or irrelevant to their lives. If an international ad is culpable in this regard, perhaps it shouldn't be on the air! Around the world, many brands have achieved great effectiveness by combining a powerful idea about themselves with creativity that excites, informs and entertains.

As markets become more competitive and brand messages less distinctive; as consumers become more exacting in their choices, ads must persuade in powerful and compelling ways with a sharp, invasive and non-negotiable voice.

It's time for a new vision. It's time for an original voice. An original voice is often a voice of dissent. It impacts and affects people and things. It is unruly and off key. It gets rebuked more than it gets rewarded. It wins no popularity contests. It is mostly celebrated in history books and lifetime achievement awards. But is invariably *intrusive, remarkable, unforgettable.*

Our mission is to invent a new language for ourselves. To sharpen our tongue. To find our voice.

Our creativity now needs to play in a larger field, in more ways and to more diverse audiences than even before. It must effectively find and communicate with those audiences wherever they are, whatever they are doing, however they feel. And this requires a collaborative mindset; a devotion to seamlessness; and the courage to integrate.

It requires leadership.

Let others waste time grading a conventional industry by conventional standards. Our time will be spent setting new standards in what we know is a new industry. Let others be foreign in their respective Towers of Babel. Our multiple, multifaceted, multichanneled voice will be seamless, will be one. And to achieve it, we must:

— Invent a new language for ourselves. Sharpen our tongue.

— Design a new voice—invasive, involving, non-negotiable.

— An immediate voice. (Leadership without urgency is self-defeating).

— An independent, inquisitive, integrated, and organically interactive voice.

— A high quality voice. (Integration without brilliance is pointless).

Our mission, market by market, discipline by discipline, is to speak with an assertive, augmented, ambitious voice. To expand our definition of creativity by expanding the quality and the reach of our work, from insights to expressions.

To embrace *Imagination*.

*"Ideas are fragile and can easily perish."*

*"Creating an idea is both an act of love and act of logic. You feel the pulse, you listen to the heartbeat."*

# What Does A
# Creative Director Do?

The world in which we live now is not the world in which we grew up. It is a very different world, made up of different values, different perceptions. The virtues of the past are the vices of the present; yesterday's heroes have become today's villains.

If you take America alone—so many of the perceptions and values we grew up with came from there—you will realize just how much the world has changed.

Take Hollywood. Once a place of film-makers, talented women and men dedicated to the task of producing magic for the silver screen. Today, a place of deal-makers, articulate women and men dedicated to the task of packaging, financing, manufacturing and distributing box office compromises.

Take Madison Avenue. Once upon a time, a place of creators, of remarkable men who gave *shape and sub*stance to our business, and whose names are still being re-arranged on the doors of agencies all over the world. Nowadays, a place of messengers, of middle-men who have bought, sold, merged and consolidated our business into what it has become: *a commodity.*

In this grave new world, advertisers are asking themselves countless questions:

— What do I sell: products, services, *brands*?

— What do I need: a brand manager, an ad manager, a marketing manager, all of the above, none of the above?

— What type of agency do I need: large or small, global or local, strategic or creative?

— Do I *really* need an agency?

— What *difference* can an agency make?

— Do I really need all these people?

— What do they actually do?

— What does the Manager do?

— What does a Creative Director do, anyway?

As an agency which believes it has the power and passion to lead the world, we must provide answers to these questions, answers which are *relevant* and *differentiated.*

We also must do it *before* the competition in order to be seen as true leaders.

Yes, Mr. Advertiser, you do sell products and you do sell services but we see your world evolving, more and more, towards *strategic brands.* Brands that *stand* for things. Brands that surface *feelings.* Brands that are bigger, warmer and closer to home than the specific products or services they represent.

It is not our prerogative, Mr. Advertiser, to determine what the best business structure for your company should be. But allow us to call your attention to the fact, more and more, that advertising decisions are being made *at the top.* Which is where we believe they *belong*; which is where we believe *we* belong.

What type of agency do you need? One with the power to be the best global and the best local agency, depending on your needs, in the markets that are important to you. One with the passion to turn insightful strategies into creative executions consumers will recognize, remember and respond to.

If your mission is to constantly improve your products and enhance your brands, then your agency's mission is to relentlessly increase your relevance to, and your *intimacy* with the Consumer.

*That* is the difference an agency can make. And that is why you should *demand* the best people it can offer.

Which brings us back to the Creative Director. These times demand a new and improved Creative Director—one who is sensitive to the changes that are taking place and capable of tackling an increasingly more challenging business environment.

There are, in my estimation, five major areas in which the Creative Director's impact is imperative.

1. The area of *Ideas:*

Ideas are probably the hardest things to come by in our business. Ideas are fragile and can easily perish. They are impossible to plan, predict or program—they happen as a product of input, instinct and inspiration. Good ones can be turned into bad ones and vice-versa. Most of the time, few people can identify a good idea and that may include the person who came up with it.

And yet, that's what our business is all about: *Ideas.*

Not just creative ideas but any idea, in any field, that will help us reach the consumer more effectively and obtain a better result for our clients.

Only those who have suffered before a blank sheet of paper understand how precious ideas are—and, therefore, how vital it is to encourage and support the people who produce them.

A Creative Director must be able to *create ideas on his or her own*. That is probably why he or she got here in the first place.

A Creative Director who remains creatively active will invariably remain able to cherish, respect, nurture and protect ideas—and therefore, able to judge them.

The good thing is, ideas come in various shapes and sizes. Some are particularly effective here and now, others will last for years. Ideas can be emotional and full of passion; ideas can be rational and purely factual. Some even manage to combine emotion and fact, which means they talk both to the heart and to the brain.

A Creative Director must be able *to work with other people's ideas*. Shape them, polish them, improve them—and still give credit where credit is due. If an idea is good, *tell them so*; if it is not good enough, *tell them why*.

A Creative Director must have the tools with which to *generate ideas:*

— the ability to examine, evaluate, accept or reject a strategy document;
— in the absence of one, the ability to provide sound strategic direction;
— the ability to cast the right talent for a project, which involves knowing one's associates and the chemistry between them;
— the ability to create the precise amount of constructiveness among creative people that will enhance the quality of the output;
— the ability to make timely use of all resources available, from within or from the outside, from home or from out-of-town, in order to get the

desired caliber of ideas.

And a Creative Director must be able *to sell ideas*. To highlight their relevance and showcase their creative content. To babysit their growth during exposure and execution; to sacrifice them when excessive interference jeopardizes their health.

*2. People:*

Our new and improved Creative Director is, by definition, a polyglot who must fluently speak and understand:
— the language which is most relevant to the Consumer he is trying to reach;
— the unstructured shorthand (and sometimes rude body language) of his Creative Staff;
— the (hopefully) articulate, precise prioritized idiom of Account Management;
— the more intellectual, food-for-thought-type language spoken by Planners and Researchers;
— the read-between-the-lines, that's not-exactly-what-we-had-in-mind language Clients sometimes utilize;
— the inscrutable variety of dialects spoken by film directors, line producers, stylists, composers, photographers and illustrators, to name but a few.

All of which boils down to people who need people in a people-driven business.

There are three groups of people Creative Director must deal with that I would like to focus on.

A Creative Director's first priority is to listen to the *consumer*.

Understanding what makes consumers tick is the most valuable contribution we can make to a client's business. Too much advertising is
created and make public without proper consumer validation and this
is one of the reasons effectiveness and relevance are so frequently under
scrutiny.

Another key priority is *creative people*. Recruiting, training,
organizing, challenging, motivating, rewarding and firing creative people—all of this a Creative Director must do.

From kidnapping the kids to seducing thy neighbor's brilliant
creative team—these are crimes of the art which we Creative Directors
must commit if we are going to succeed in attracting better people and
creating better advertising.

And if we are going to *motivate* people and make them feel good
about working with us, we must offer them something beyond simply a
job. We must give them a sense of what the future might bring. A career
path. We must be prepared to be specific about it: if you perform, this is
how far you can go. This approach appeals to people's sense of long-term
achievement, and as a result, generates loyalty.

Whatever we do, we must keep a hand in. Whatever led you to
your Creative Director position, keep doing it.

It is reassuring for the people in your department that you can
perform your craft well and that you take pleasure in it. It is also a reminder—to them—that their leader can do it just as well, or better, should
the need occur.

Motivating by example hardly ever fails.

And when reward time comes, celebrate, support your people.
Reach out and praise someone. Speak up. Make a public announcement.
Write a congratulatory note. Gather the troops. Make a 2 am phone call.

Open a bottle of champagne. Sing, shout. Promote someone. Declare a holiday.

The message is—a Creative Director should celebrate all victories, no matter how small. Fuel the passion. And when defeated, be constructive, find out what went wrong and what needs to be fixed. Outline a new plan of attack. Above all, be supportive of your team. Just make sure they gave their best shot. Anything else is unacceptable.

A Creative Director should *hire slowly and fire quickly*. How many times have we hired someone we weren't totally sure of because we needed to solve a pressing problem. How often do we take the time to have a candidate interviewed by more than one decision maker?

Conversely, how many times have we perpetuated mediocrity and allowed someone to stay too long?

How often have we resort to transfer an employee because we didn't want a confrontation.

This behavior is not only a sign of weak creative management—it actually works against the objective of motivating the good people we have, the ones we want to keep and groom.

A Creative Director must be able to work with his business partners within the agency: the Account Director, the Research and/or Strategic Planning Director, the Media Director—and, of course, the Manager.

Let's face it: the days of *prima donnas* and *empty suits* are gone. Reality is—some of the most successful Creative Directors in the business are people who have been able *to bridge the disciplines*, thus moving on to a higher level of professionalism. What these relationships require is work. Chemistry can be *worked at*. Differences of opinion can be *worked out*. And when it comes to solving a crisis or pitching a new piece of business, nothing beats good, old-fashioned *teamwork.*

### 3. Our *Craft:*

The new improved Creative Director is ten times more demanding, from a craft point-of-view, than his or her predecessor.

He or she will not allow a half-baked idea to be presented on the basis that a film director will fix it during the shoot.

He or she will not allow the use of executional device to hide the absence of an idea. By the same token, he or she will not allow an established, precious Brand Equity to be tampered with in the name of irresponsibly breaking the mold.

To responsibly break the mold one must understand what is being broken and be able to replace it with something that is substantially superior from a creative viewpoint. It also helps to realize that a new mold has just been created which will have to be broken in the future.

The one thing to keep an eye on is the caliber of our craft contribution.

Are our writers and art directors truly searching for the best idea or are they happy to go with the ones that will sell—the path of least resistance? Is our argument—whether it is expressed in words, pictures or sounds—well constructed and persuasive and memorable? What about our words, pictures and sounds? Are they fresh? Is there substance in them? Will they trigger a response? Did we create them for the consumer or for the creative community around us?

Our new and improved Creative Directors understand that there is no contradiction between protecting existing brand equity and pursuing creative excellence.

He and she understand that *Not Invented Here* must be replaced by *Now Improved Here*. Above all, they hire, fire, train, groom, challenge, judge and reward with one objective in mind: *to publish the best ad we can craft,* not just the one that we can sell.

4. *Money:*

Money, except that which comes in the form of a paycheck, has always been an ugly word with Creative People.

"All they think about is money. There is excessive concern with the bottom line", Creative Directors used to say.

"Money is too important to be left in the hands of creative people", Managers used to say.

As a result, an intricate system of checks and balances has evolved, over the years, making the movement and usage of money in an agency very difficult indeed.

Truth is—money is an integral part of our lives and today's Creative Director has had to learn to deal with it and put it to good use. In fact, I have come to believe money is too important to be left exclusively in the hands of financial people!

Why?

Because we must be able to hire good people—and that means *investing* money.

We must compensate people in a responsible, yet competitive fashion—and that means *managing* money.

We must be able to tell whether our clients are getting value for money when the estimates come in—which means *controlling money.*

We must be conscious of the need to control expenses and make a profit (this is, after all, a business)—that means *making* money.

In addition to understanding the consumer, attracting and motivating talented people, generating and executing memorable ideas and selling them to Clients, we also must know how to invest, manage, control and make *money*.

The message is clear: yes, you need to be accountable and profitable—that is how and why you have become Creative Directors. But do not—ever again!—allow yourselves to be intimidated by the subject of money. You are just as responsible for it as your counterparts in Management and you have the right to fight for what you believe is the most constructive use of it.

*5. Atmosphere:*

Flowers have trouble growing in the desert. And a Creative Department must have an atmosphere that is conducive to the blossoming of good ideas.

For years I thought there was something magic about atmosphere. Something clicked and there it was—people felt good, creative ideas flowed easily, Clios and Gold Lions and new assignments poured in!

Over time, I learned that there are a couple of logical, practical things that you can do to help create a good atmosphere.

Start with an attitude—your attitude towards work, people and ideas. Let them know how you feel.

A poker face will never win you passion or respect or loyalty. Sitting on a fence will not motivate anybody into making more of an effort.

If you are upset, show it. And explain it. You would be amazed at how well people can take rational, constructive criticism.

Then structure for personal growth.

Structure your department in such a way that people know where they can go next and what they should aim for. There's nothing more conducive to lack of interest and poor productivity than lack of future perspective.

In doing this, try and be sensitive to chemistry. Organization charts look good on paper but they are worthless if the invisible lines of chemistry are not in place. In that regard, I have learned that small and integrated pockets of creative activity tend to work better than elaborate schemes which separate the various crafts as in an assembly line. In other words, let writers art direct, art directors produce and producers create—if they feel like it.

Those of you who run smaller agencies know exactly what I am talking about—you have been doing it for years. It is those in the larger agencies that must be mindful of the fact that creativity is not an industrial process—it is totally dependent on how people get on with each other.

With a good structure in place, you are now prepared to lead.

Which means you collect opinions, not votes. Votes invariably lead to consensus, and consensus runs the risk of being the lowest common denominator.

People appreciate leadership. They need it, expect it and respond to it. They want to become leaders themselves.

What you want from them is input that will help you make a decision; you do not want them to make the decision for you.

You may find it helps to *keep it lean and mean.*

Trim the excess fat. Accept a touch more workload than you are able to carry. Generate an atmosphere of productive activity with little or no room for idleness. Turn down unreasonable deadlines but never take more time than you need to complete a task.

Keeping it lean and mean will decrease the politics and increase teamwork.

All of which adds to a healthier, more passionate working environment.

Don't make promises you can't keep.

In other words, shoot straight:

— Have frank discussions with your people.

— Prepare through evaluations of their performance and share these with them.

— Establish goals for people to achieve, let them know how they are doing.

— Make sure they know where they stand.

Above all, do not promise rewards you cannot deliver.

In my book, the imperatives facing the new and improved Creative Director therefore are:

Creative Imperative One: the generation, evaluation, protection and enhancement of our most tangible product: *Ideas.*

Creative Imperative Two: the understanding, development and skillful management of our most valuable asset: *People.*

Creative Imperative Three: the command and optimum use of our most influential skill: our *Craft.*

Creative Imperative Four: the mature and realistic understanding of *Money:* as a tool and as a goal.

Creative Imperative Five: the design, construction and careful maintenance of an exciting creative *Atmosphere.*

I know some of the above is obvious; I hope some of it is fresh. All of it is what a Creative Director *does* or *should do.*

The difference is—I firmly believe a Creative Director can do it better.

*"Great ads are born
of great strategies. Great strategies are born of great insights."*

# Destination: Reputation

World leadership in creativity will not come just from doing superior work, but also—because perception is reality—from being recognized for doing so. The world is full of people who are legends in their own minds. We want to be leaders in our time. We want the claim and the fame!

Understanding the problem to be solved should be the foundation of any advertising, especially if it is to be superior advertising. Too many ads today provide answers to questions you haven't asked.

Good interrogators always get to the truth. Or to a truth that is intrinsic to a product and relevant to its users.

That leads us to the *solution*.

The strategic problem should be solved before creative begins. It sounds obvious and logical but it is not the way it always works.

How many ads have you seen, lately, that seem in desperate search of a strategy?

It's like meeting someone who knows how to talk, but doesn't know what to say!

In our interrogation process, it pays to isolate a fact. And I don't necessarily mean a fact fact. A feeling is a fact. A belief is a fact. A value is a fact. An ability, an attitude. Soul can be a fact. Maybe we need or even have more than one fact. Two, three facts. The operating word here is isolate—as in focus on, concentrate.

Creatives should think before they act—have directions before the creative process begins. To seek breakthrough information and breakthrough insights to help guide the creative process.

There's no creative leadership without strategic leadership.

Let's look at the *target*.

So many people, in so many niches, with so many choices and so many channels.

I am referring to genuine expressions of preference, taste, personality, attitude, lifestyle, which co-exist within one person, within one day.

I am referring to the need to move people and make sales at different levels: rational, emotional, practical. Share of mind, share of heart, share of guts. Share of wallet, share of hormones. Share of hair, share of throat, share of driving pleasure. Share of Summer, share of Christmas, share of Saturday night.

I am referring to the need to acknowledge, understand and address many constituencies within the framework of one brand, one idea. Share of young, share of old. Share of black, share of green, share of blue collar. Asians, Islamics, Hispanics, demographics, dialects.

Your client's budget cannot afford to reach them. Your client's sales forecast cannot afford not to reach them. You cannot afford to either neglect them or single them out or ignore them, or God forbid, alienate them.

What's the creative department to do?

You start with an Idea. Then you look for relevant ways to express it. Words can help.

If you are trying to sell an idea, words do it best. If an idea is truly fresh, it couldn't borrow from existing images, anyway.

Remember: we are trying to be leaders. Suffice it to say that consumers are exercising judgment, are seeking specificity. They want ads to help them make their choices.

Consumers want clarity, clients want contact. We can help both by ensuring that the product, the brand, *is always central to the idea.*

We can help them both by knowing and using the words, the idioms spoken by the various constituencies they need to reach.

But perhaps the most awesome challenge for creative people who wish to lead the way is to continuously impact the human eye with original, relevant and memorable *images.*

The reason to attend festivals is so you can see what not to do. It is to imagine ways to go beyond what you see. The reason to meet with directors is to enlist them in your quest for effective originality.

Your best friends? You own two eyes. Your instincts. Your integrity. Your resourcefulness.

Trends? Start your own. So long as you are able to "stir desire and impel action," to use the words of one H.K.McCann, to foster them, not to follow them.

And once you hit, hit it good, hit it long—and then run, because there will be hundreds of guys following your trend.

Which means: more than ever, we must know what we are selling. This isn't just about the nature and quality of the idea itself, it's about how to sell it. An analysis of our industry reveals that many creative people tend to spend the bulk of their presentation time describing the location, the casting, the wardrobe, the shooting style, the editorial pace and the music beat before they explain the idea and how it fulfills the strategy.

For many years I was accused of overselling. Mr. Oversell.

And when the final product didn't live up to my presentation, there was hell to pay. I learned it the hard way. I then became cautiously enthusiastic in my salesmanship and unreasonably demanding of final production.

So, pick the best people to be your strategic alliances. They are there to complement and supplement the insights, the accuracy, the intimacy with a client's problem that only the creative person has. In the process, cover all angles: this expression, that framing, this alternate gesture, that tighter product shot.

In these days of mattes and special effects, very few people realize how much of the creative process takes place at post-production.

Do we do enough? No such thing as enough. There is no finish line in the creative process—there will always be a better line of dialogue, a funnier ending, a better shot, a tighter cut, a clearer mix, a better performance—and it is our obligation to get them.

The thing to remember is: our reputation rides on every ad we write, produce and publish. Every single ad counts. An inferior ad will pull us down. A superior ad will pull us up. That is why good enough is definitely not good enough. An ad should never be termed ready until it is really good. Better still, until it is great.

More and more, creative leadership has to do with the *size* of the idea. Clients need ideas they can spread across all communications channels, no matter how unconventional.

We all know what this means to Media people: it means they have to wear their lateral thinking hats again.

To creative people, this means forgetting their personal reels and books for a moment and trying to expand their thinking. It means contributing to packaging, events, merchandising, promotions and every conceivable expression a brand or product can benefit from:

— above the line;

— below the line;

— over time;

— over borders;

— every which way.

There are advertising people who believe their job is done when they deliver a finished ad or commercial to a publication or broadcaster.

As professionals, our job is not done until we have created energy; until we have moved men and women into stores and products into homes; until we've made sales.

To be the best and to be recognized as such.

Passive behavior will not engender recognition, active behavior will. How can we actively showcase ourselves?

First, let's make sure we are seen for the totality of what we do and not just for one or two accounts.

Second, we must give ourselves a License To Dare, a mechanism by which all fear of innovative thinking is removed. We must persuade clients to expect the unexpected and not punish the agency for bringing it to the table. This should provide new ideas with sequential green lights inside the agency as well.

Lastly, we must advertise the advertising, be it through winning awards, creating pro-bono ads, speaking at universities or exposing it to our own colleagues at the agency.

A very effective means of establishing a creative reputation is to volunteer to do public service work. While less stressful and less demanding than everyday client work, public service does provide the agency with a highly creative outlet and does capture the imagination of the creative community.

Creative Leadership is not just a matter of professional pride, it's a matter of business survival. We must lead to be able to continue to grow.

In order to lead we must win. Every reputable award show, every visible advertising festival in which we win adds fuel to the fire. Every client award we win, every recognition counts.

Yes, we want to be famous for our size and business performance.

Yes, we want to be famous for our professionalism, our coverage, our grasp of cultures.

Above all, we want to be famous for the brands we help build and for the sales we help close.

One last word about ideas:

Ideas are not the exclusive province of the Creative Department. They can, have and will come from any department in the agency, further enhancing our reputation as creators of relevant and original solutions for our clients.

*"We want to be leaders in our time. We want the claim and the fame!"*

*"Communication isn't what you say, it's what people understand."*

# Put A Brain
# In Your Campaign

It is important to understand that advertising is an expression.

It expresses a corporate destination and corporate desires.

It expresses a brand's identity and a brand's intention.

It expresses the relevance, timelessness and advantages of product offerings.

Advertising isn't an isolated act. It cohabits with all other dynamics of the marketing process at a given point in time in a given place. It acknowledges the current culture of consumers, the culture of the category it is attempting to impact, and the culture of the brand itself.

Advertising builds bridges. It seeks to connect the principal in the marketing process such as the consumer, the advertiser, the trade and all other relevant constituencies. Advertising agencies—as well as other disciplines in the communications arena—are therefore the bridge builders between these audiences.

Advertising is about ideas. If all your advertising agency gives you today is an execution, look for another agency. It is the ability to generate ideas that differentiates advertising agencies from production companies.

Who knows where ideas come from? Authorship is one of the most elusive concepts of modern creativity and that is particularly true in the advertising business. Awards books are packed with credit lists, which often take more space than the awarded pieces themselves.

Yet, there is great reluctance to discuss this issue of authorship, because a significant portion of it is outsourced. While it is acceptable to outsource the services of directors, illustrators, photographers and composers, the industry avoids the debate about idea generation. As if there's a firewall, and absolutely no blur whatsoever, between the conceptual and the executional.

That's the rub: how do I explain to others, how do I explain to myself, that I use freelance help?

If the movie and music businesses are any indication, it matters more that the ideas are powerful, memorable and successful; and less, the type of collaboration that designed them. Historical fact: commissioned artists actually pre-date in-house creators.

An agency is judged by a multitude of skills. Its grasp of the mission. Its knowledge: brand, product, consumer, competition. Its deftness at designing strategies. The imaginative skills to convert all this into compelling communication.

A client expects its communication to be effective and famous; and wants to know that the idea comes from the core of the agency. That it is something the agency has a passion for and will stake its reputation on. In this context, how the agency arrives at ideas is its own concern.

Most outsourcing is borne out of need. A particular skill is needed. Category experience can speed up the process.

A lot is caused by the imponderable of the day: accounts lost or gained; budget cuts; shifting airdates etc. Not surprisingly, it is all in how it is used.

Ideas come from insights, ingenuity, inspiration, innovation.

Without consumer insights there is no direction.

Without ingenuity there is no differentiation.

Without inspiration there is no interest.

Without innovation there is no impact.

An idea is a child. The last thing it needs is rejection—it kills the idea and alienates the parent. Instead, ideas should be nurtured, shaped, reprimanded if necessary, but given an opportunity to grow. When conceived rightly from the start, even small ideas can grow to become big ones.

Outsourcing that merely fills a gap or handles a crunch, without adequate briefing, supervision and follow-through, deserves a bad name. Ditto, freelancers who bring in their hard drives, the old, unsold ideas from their last gig.

The smart agency is that which embraces and empowers the talent; marshals it as part of the overall effort; surrounds it with the appropriate knowledge, tools and direction; allows it to see its own work to fruition; that agency and its clients stand to win.

The purpose of advertising ideas is to sell. Moving products off the shelf, changing an existing perception, budding a feeling towards a brand, attracting a new audience, offering a service—softly or hardly, ideas must sell. Effecting sales does not come from advertising alone—many tools are required to accomplish the task.

Continuity breeds confidence. Once you have a relevant idea, born out of a relevant consumer insight—no brain, no gain!—stick with it and execute it in various ways, across various channels to endure not only continued sales but continued trust. After all, everything communicates.

Ideas and tools are important at all times. But they are fundamental in crisis or in a recession. They will determine the difference between a problem and an opportunity. Your idea will keep your brand vibrant and relevant through the difficult time. Your toolkit will give you the flexibility to address transactional and tactical issues to ensure sales and survival.

I believe in *work that works, work that wins.* By that I mean effectiveness in reaching and persuading consumers about our clients' brands, products and services—as well as earning visibility in the marketplace via peer recognition, valuable press coverage, winning awards. And we believe the way to get to *work that works, work that wins* is hard-work, brain-work, modernity in our execution, relentless consistency in our delivery.

Creating an idea is both an act of love and act of logic. You feel the pulse, you listen to the heartbeat.

You gather facts, you draw the conclusions, you write a strategy. Now you must build the bridge, nurture the child—and that can only be done through creativity and consistency.

*"Products and brands may have a universal marketing strategy, but advertising is still language—still a manifestation—it must be relevant in order to work"*

*"After two decades, global communications are alive and well except they now live in people's hearts and minds, not in maps or charts."*

# Borderless Creativity

## Not Multinational: Multicultural

As geographic borders and language barriers become less important, other forms of culture come into play and affect the successful development of global communications:

— The Culture of the Consumer
   (historical, ethnic, religious)
— Popular Culture
— The Corporate Culture
— The Culture of the Category
— The Culture of the Brand

This is a technique for transforming consumer information into consumer insight. It is a process for gathering, decoding and expressing consumer sentiments to make our ads the most effective. It immerses us in the milieu and mindset of the target consumer. It entails engagement in an incessant dialogue with consumers, whether through group of individual interviews, and constant analysis of the context surrounding consumers, their environment, their media consumption, their purchasing trends, and so on. With this approach we can go beyond targets and strategies based solely on demographic or other statistical data, and we can focus on real-world considerations such as life stages, like-mindedness and the role of media consumption patterns in defining audience attitudes.

Life Stage Global Constituencies:

— Identity Builders
— Career Builders
— Family Builders
— New Life Builders

— Identity Builders: The ads most liked by teenagers around the world don't have overt, rational selling messages for products, but instead tend to associate a brand with an entertaining and engaging scenario. They tend to have a clear beginning, middle and end; often incorporate action, high-tech adventure, occasionally even sex; they unfold like an action movie or a video game sequence.

Favorite themes include rebellion against authority and a mocking of political correctness. This rebellion isn't angry like that of past generations; instead, it pokes fun at issues believed to be taken too seriously by society.

Despite the many high-tech, fantasy-like environments in Identity Builder advertising, the spots most enjoyed often celebrate a sense of realness, honesty and human imperfection.

— Career Builders: Preferred commercials are clever, ironic and metaphorical and make biting points about issues of interest to

Career Builders—namely, what it takes to succeed.

Many Career-Builders' favorite spots deal tangentially with job-related issues but none actually feature people at work, tapping into the idea that a career is built with brains and talent, not time logged in an office.

A clear theme in the ads favored by Career Builders: success does not come from old-fashioned achievement. A career is about being independent and self-motivated, and it's more about lifestyle and attitude than a job title.

In addition to ironic situation and dialogue, Career Builders' favorite ads tend to employ a lot of interesting and artistic visuals and music.

— Family Builders: Ads enjoyed by Family Builders differ sharply from market to market. This is largely due to the different roles of women and mother in different cultures.

In more traditional or emerging markets, Family Builders most liked standard product-benefit ads for household products. Mothers using products in nurturing family environments, receiving appreciation in return.

In more progressive or developed markets, mothers favored more entertaining and sophisticated ads. Although the product categories were similar to those in more traditional markets, the style was less direct. The favorite ads in progressive markets rely more on humor and special effects and are less likely to show a family scenario.

— New Life Builders: Unlike the more visually-oriented ads enjoyed by younger generations, New Life Builders tend to prefer a lot of dialogue and articulate conversation. They enjoy ads featuring current celebrities, risqué situations and off-color humor. The ads clearly show a vitality of spirit.

Many ads support the notion that age gives New Life Builders greater perspective, but it doesn't make them irrelevant. Whatever the connection with the younger generation, it is not one of dependency. New Life Builders are frequently portrayed in the favorite ads as self-reliant and successful.

Based on their choice of favorite commercials, New Life Builders see themselves as strong, perhaps not physical, but in the sense that they have achieved a level of wisdom and financial stability.

Message, Delivery and Style:

— Teens like straightforward storytelling that is heavy on action and light on dialogue.

— Career Builders favor subtler and cleverly delivered messages, often that take the form of metaphors. They like a strong mix of visuals, music and dialogue.

— Family Builders in emerging markets prefer straightforward product/benefit demonstrations; those in developed markets are gravitating to more sophisticated, entertaining ads.

— New Life Builders favor ads with well articulated dialogue, as well as the occasional slapstick humor.

*"Creativity is everybody's job:*
*substance, relevance, brilliance, endurance.*
*Sequential green lights for innovative thinking."*

*"Definition of effective communication:
compelling advertising that builds or
reinforces a bond between Consumers and Brands,
with something substantial to tell, told brilliantly."*

# Change, Trends &
# The Future Of Advertising

1. *Change* has always been defined as alteration; the exchange of one thing for another; a fresh outlook; the passing from one form, phase, place or state to another.

And in our business—as dynamic and mercurial as it is—change happened at a pace, almost predictable, always evolutionary. Until recently, that is.

Change has now been modified by another little word, *speed.* Rate of motion; the magnitude of velocity irrespective of its direction; the rate at which something proceeds or is done.

It is no coincidence that the word speed is also used to describe a stimulant, a drug.

So, *change is not what it used to be.*

It's more challenging, less logical, more disturbing, less orderly than ever before. All the do's and don'ts of the business went out the window. There's a new consumer to be understood. New ways to reach that consumer. New idioms to speak. New technologies to learn and apply. A new client mind set. New business realities. New professional choices.

The advertising agency business is going through it's *mid-life cri-*

*sis.* Let's hope it doesn't come out of it weakened and intimidated but bold and daring and rejuvenated.

2. We see the emergence of a new phenomenon, which we've chosen to call *the new globalism.*

Whereas global used to mean one sight, one sound, one sell—often centrally designed and centrally produced—the new globalism is about *ideas that work* regardless of where they come from.

Whereas global used to mean Western Europe, North America and a handful of mature societies in other continents, the new globalism stands for a world of converging attitudes everywhere, including Eastern Europe, India, Indonesia, Indochina, Africa, the Middle East and Latin America.

It is a world of *convergence.* It is a world in which *cultural nuance* makes a tangible difference. And a world in which *no-one* has exclusivity on creativity.

3. I think the agency business has been taught a lesson in humility. For a while, agency people walked around talking about partnership and being custodians of their clients' brands and such. We are in the service business and our job is to come up with a good *strategy,* a good *idea* and a good *expression* of it.

It's that basic, that simple.

Agency brass learned that time spent on a client's business is more important than time spent on mergers and acquisitions. Creative people learned that *everything is a medium* worth exploring and that new media are there to be embraced and mastered, not to be sneezed at and ignored.

I learned to broaden my definition of creativity beyond writing and producing ads. I used it to manage people, to manage relationships, to help our clients grow their businesses, at whatever level.

4. Gradually, and not without some trepidation, we are becoming more horizontal, less controlled, more lateral, less measured. I mean: unplugged. Tough to do, especially when you are big and somewhat set in your ways—but absolutely necessary, essential to survival and future growth. I see it, however, as an organic and spontaneous event—not some pre-meditated, pre-fabricated formula for the agency of the future. As far as I am concerned, *life is virtual enough.*

5. Unfortunately, some of the new technologies are having more impact on advertising than advertising is having on them. Most agency people have chosen to act like the proverbial ostrich with its head stuck in the sand, rather than embrace and master these new tools, applying to them the same creative energy and adrenalin they put into conventional advertising. This is particularly true of creative people, who somehow find it difficult to migrate from the cozy little world of print ads and television commercials to the intimidating technological universe.

6. I will make one prediction and one wish. My prediction is that the boundaries that currently separate the various facets of communications—from public relations to advertising to entertainment—will eventually blur and a world of *applied creativity* will emerge. In this world, two people will rule: the person with *imagination* and the person with *the remote control.* My wish is that humanity will wake up and realize that the news is not part of the entertainment.

*"In this new world, there is a language out there for which there isn't a dictionary yet."*

# Change & Global Advertising

There is change all around us.

Business has changed quite dramatically. Aspiring globals have become truly global. Heretofore locals have developed global aptitudes. Established globals have been slowed down by the strong headwinds of lifestyle relevance, nationalism and poor press.

New technologies, convergence, e-commerce and dot-coms (not to mention perennials such as mergers and acquisitions) have become the lexicon and syntax of a brave new world of business, where Wall Street, not cultural currency, reigns supreme.

People have changed, but less than we think. They still wake up, brush their teeth, eat breakfast, go where they need to go, do what they need to do, return to base, eat and drink, play and entertain themselves—go to bed again. They travel, shop, make choices, have sex, have children, absorb and exude data, buy and sell things—through new channels, perhaps; more contemporary methods of payment, perhaps; seduced by a less innocent, more cynical selling message, perhaps; but in the end it is still about "how do I improve the way that I feel right now" (not "today" or "these days", or "in general", but "right now", as distinct from "a minute ago", or even "a minute from now").

The world, as we used to know it, has actually seen substantially change, but most of us have barely scratched the surface of that change. Our ground level view is, by definition, immediate, incomplete, unfocused. Blurred. It takes time and perspective to develop a sharper, clearer picture. From a marketplace point of view, countries have transformed into constituencies. Constituencies are defined not by age, not by sex, not by language, not by color—or any such conventional criteria—but by the way they think and the way they act. Call it like-minded constituencies. They inhabit a borderless world. In this world, film, TV, music, data and the news don't go through passport control. In this world, there is a language out there for which there isn't a dictionary yet. A fluid, fickle language, subject to manipulation and interpretation. A language in which words have given way to icons.

What is near may never be visited; what is far can be accessed at a moment's notice. Choice isn't about having choice, it is about believing there is a choice. Showrooms and supermarket shelves and e-commerce websites are landscapes surrounding a choice that, in many cases has already been made.

Money isn't necessarily an object. That is what it has become, an object. Having it is a present tense proposition, not a long-term preoccupation. Consumption habits start with what media you consume. In a world geographically and economically borderless, emotional borders rule.

In this New Globalism, where the conventional lines of demarcation between what's local and what's global are drawn in quicksand, the opportunities for Global Brands abound.

They are the oasis, the idyllic island to which to gravitate. The mission, for the Global Brands that choose to accept it, will be to relentlessly predict how consumers will feel—and, consequently, act—next. As opposed to obsessively dissect how they felt and acted yesterday. Thus equipped, they will need to interact with those consumers in the most relevant, most creative and effective manner. They will need to:

— *recognize* the culture of the Category;

— *reflect* the culture of the Brand;

— *respect* the culture of the Consumer, a list which must be amended to include a 4th R;

— *respond* to the culture of the Mindset.

A Global Brand that does it credibly and compellingly, faster and better that the other guy, will prosper. Locally and globally, as these terms of the past increasingly become one and the same.

Enter... *The Borderless Brand*

We have come a long way since the days of a centrally-produced, locally translated, one-ad-fits-all approach to global advertising. Brand ideas that can literally come from anywhere and travel anywhere have a new power—primarily because many so-called developing markets around the world have become as sophisticated and complex as the countries that used to send them advertising.

Among other things, the industry has learned that not all brands or product categories lend themselves to global communication. Take beer, for example. Even though beers are consumed on similar occasions, for similar reasons, by similar consumers—in most of the world—no single beer brand has yet managed to establish itself as the leading global beer. Beer is still different, culture to culture.

The industry has learned that relevance to consumers must be the first and foremost criterion in determining whether a brand should act as local brand, a regional brand or a global brand.

Advertisers have become more sophisticated and no longer adopt the global stance for the wrong reasons: control, economies of scale, etc. The word global has been misused, overused.

There is the global airline, the global credit card, the global newspaper, the global network, the global everything.

There is a global housewife, a global teenager, a global new car buyer, a global senior citizen, a global everybody.

The word global has been abused.

Advertising for certain brands, in certain categories, can be more global than for certain others.

The global thinking has given way to a much more complex and sophisticated behavioral map, which cannot be ignored.

The truth is, there has been an evolution from the simplistic, one-size-fits all global view to what I prefer to refer to as multicultural advertising. In other words, advertising that is sensitive to cultural traits and viewers' attitudes; advertising that tries to seduce its audience rather than satisfy a corporate agenda.

But, as outrageous as this my sound, the world isn't that simple anymore. Historical events have re-shaped the world, have re-shaped people's perceptions and priorities.

Advertising, as we know, does not live in a vacuum. Products and brands may have a universal marketing strategy, but advertising is still language—still a manifestation—and as such it must be relevant in order to work.

But the world *multicultural* isn't restricted solely to chunks of geography and historical heritage. In the creative world of advertising, there are other *cultures* that come into play:

—The *culture of the category* (does your product or brand define it or is it one among many?)

—The *culture of the brand* itself (what does it stand for? What does it do best for its heavy user?)

—The *culture of your target audience* (trusting senior citizen, sarcastic young adults, young housewives, etc?)

Successful multicultural advertisers do not necessarily run the same execution in every market. They consistently convey the same idea about their products and brands. They convey the same idea through every available channel, from television commercials to match boxes.

Successful multicultural advertisers do not choose the multicultural approach to save production money. They do so in order to impart a cohesive, consistent, controlled idea about their products and brands.

Successful multicultural advertisers understand that a culture isn't defined by *borders* or *language*, anymore, it is defined by mindset, feelings and context.

Products and brands do not communicate to *places*, they communicate with *people*. Communication isn't what you say, it's what people understand. To speak someone's language is to appeal to them, to become close. Few advertisers truly understand that it really isn't about the technology, the work ethic or the track record—it's about one-on-one identification.

Provided consumer relevance can be achieved, the motivation for global behavior should be the dissemination of a consistent and cohesive idea about a brand. Brands, after all, are supposed to simplify the lives of consumers. A brand that speaks with one, relevant voice, should make the buying decision process even simpler.

But perhaps one of the most important lessons of the last decade or so—especially when it comes to advertising agencies—is the realization that global means *intimacy* with many cultures, not mere *presence* in many countries.

What we are now seeing is the emergence of a new type of globalism where the *idea* rules and ideas can come from anywhere. If an idea touches consumers, perhaps it also travels well. If it travels well, why confine it to one place.

*"Brands do not communicate to places,*
*Brands communicate with people."*

*"Make my brand central.*
*Make my product central.*
*Avoid advertising purely as an art form,*
*with no consequences to the product or brand being advertised.*
*Consumers expect advertising to help them*
*make decisions, rationally or emotionally or both.*
*They expect clarity. I am not arguing for hard-sell;*
*I am arguing against the absence of sell."*

# The Power Of Brands

What I believe you and I and anyone who is trying to manage a Brand should remember is—Brands are difficult *to manage and very easy to mismanage.*

To manage a Brand you need *to respect its past, nurture its present and plan for its future.*

If you betray what Brand has historically stood for, you will fail. If you fail to see its growth opportunities—through logical extensions, through constant evolution—you will not succeed. But if you succeed in charting a course for it that is both safe and ambitious, you stand a good chance of perpetuating it.

Harder than *to reinvent a Brand's personality and presentation*—in other words, to celebrate your arrival, leave your mark—is to *resist the temptation* to tamper with something people have learned to *trust* and *recognize* and *reach for.*

If I neglect a Brand's potential for a larger role in the lives of Consumers, I will cripple it. If I extend it beyond the credibility and acceptability of Consumers, I could kill it.

The explanation for all this is very simple.

Once a legitimate Brand is created and developed, it no longer belongs to its creator or temporary manager. It belongs to its users and heavy users—to its loyal Consumers. Because it simplifies the lives of Consumers, it lives in their hearts and minds, their impulses and memories and shopping lists.

And that's not just the best place for a Brand to be. It is the *only* place.

For thousands of years, goods and services have been known and rated according to their provenance. Where they came from. Who brought them to the market. In time, pride of provenance—what is referred to today as a reputation—became the distinguishing factor between products and services of a similar type, of the same category. Competition came into existence even before money ever changed hands, when barter was the principal means of transaction. To simplify choice, a new and practical commercial language emerged, which served the dual purpose of protecting provenance, as well as extolling the virtues of products and services and highlighting the difference between them, in an effort to educate and persuade prospective users.

That language is what is known today as Branding.

Brands have existed for as long as anyone alive can remember and are a viral part of the everyday life of everyone.

What started as a mark—indicating ownership, or craftsmanship, or both—ultimately became a trademark, all to guide and influence buyers when choosing what to buy. In time, the consistency of delivery of certain trademarks earned them a valuable following, which became known as customer loyalty, and a key landmark in the evolution, in marketing terms, from trademarks to Brands.

Trademarks that offered more than the mere product information and expressed unique features or characteristics; consistently high quality standards; social recognition and/or admiration; aesthetics and durability; and when required, fast and reliable maintenance; money-back and performance guarantees; etc,—earned their way into the homes, and into the hearts of consumers. Beyond appreciating the tangible attributes of certain trademarks, consumers actually granted them values, both rational and emotional.

Although not an official anniversary, the granting of values to trademarks signaled the birthday of modern Brands.

Brands became, therefore, living entities, complete with personal histories, personality traits, credibility and trust limitations accepted and expected behavior patterns, extended families, offspring of their own. Brands came to possess their own DNA, as defined by their origin and design, their management over time, their relationship with consumers. While the human DNA is a unique, immutable sequence of characteristics, Brand DNA is malleable, manageable, adjustable to the times and tastes it seeks to impact.

Many Brands have derived great benefit from possessing a very clear DNA—and from having skillfully managed its various components over time, and across geographies, age groups and differing socio-economic constituencies. The globalization of the economy has, if anything, fueled Brand globalization; Brands, in turn, have leaned heavily on their perceived personae—their DNA—to also succeed across cultures.

Most leading Brands succeed because of their clear and unequivocal DNA, that facet among facets that best defines the Brands core competency and primary purpose:
— it declares its ethos;
— it bespeaks its values;

— it exudes its personality;

— it celebrates its uniqueness.

Future success, however, will depend on the Brand's ability to remain true to and/or evolve that DNA:

— Brands have a DNA;

— corporations have a DNA;

— a Brand's DNA is not guaranteed;

— a DNA is not built overnight.

To successfully market a Brand's DNA is to establish and exploit a compelling connection between its specialness and the core desire of its most likely constituency.

To successfully globalize a Brand's DNA is to elevate and expand that connection beyond geography, nationalism and cultural identity, in search of like-minded constituencies.

Managing DNA today:

— well defined core competency;

— well defined, like-minded constituency;

— compelling, unique personality;

— virtual, real-time consumer insights;

— imaginative insight interpretation;

— organic interactive capability;

— a lifestyle enhancement, not a cultural infringement.

Country of origin can be an essential ingredient of a Brand's DNA.

In the world of Global Brands, nationality is an added enticement, a reinforcement of provenance, a statement of cultural genuineness—valuable and enduring assets when competing in cross-border categories. Brands that travel and behave as guests of the cultures they are trying to seduce—tend to succeed, more often than not.

Brands that feel entitled to travel on the strength of their prominence at home; that apply the home formula without an effort to understand and address the audience to which it is intended are prone to fail, more often than not. There is a little or no room for patriotism in Global Brand building. Pride of provenance, the very foundation of Trademarks and Brands since the beginning of commerce, is best expressed when products are positioned as a lifestyle enhancement, not a cultural infringement.

Managing a Brand is also an act of logic and act of love. You gather the facts, you draw the conclusions, you write the strategy. You choose the tools and you exact the budget. Only now you must build that bridge, nurture that child—and that can only be done through creativity and continuity.

*"Focus on what's real:*
*Clients are real. Brands are real. Competition is real.*
*Eliminate the distractions—*
*and focus our best*
*people on the real needs of our Clients.*
*That's where the Growth is."*

# Save The Brands

I learned in this business that if you can touch a nerve in a meaningful way, you will make a sale.

I don't dwell in the past. Every time I board a plane to Asia I get the feeling I am going back to the future.

I am not haunted by the celebrated controversy around the subject of global advertising. In fact, I believe global advertising already is our communications environment—or at least a substantial portion of it. Of course people will continue to be different—that's what gives them *character, individuality*. But because they are also human, their similarities will be greater and greater.

What I am haunted by is the phenomenon I've chosen to call "endangered species syndrome". It has made dinosaurs extinct. It has made bald eagles very rare indeed. In the course of history, it has affected every facet of life on our planet, from animals to plants to minerals; from empires to entire civilizations; from military tactics to political theories; from writing instruments to automobiles; from rules of conduct to basic human values.

What I am haunted by is the ever-increasing sensation that this most unique of marketing inventions—The Brand—is the latest victim of the "endangered species syndrome."

To begin with, they just don't seem to make them like they used to. With a few, notable exceptions, state-of-the-art Brands are a bit too mechanical; a bit too non-specific; cold rather than warm; and it is going to take some time until they become trustworthy. Until they begin to trigger images in people's minds.

But even worse is what seems to be happening with the Good Old Brands. The Brands that *stood* for things. The Brands that surfaced *feelings*. The Brands that were bigger, warmer and closer to home than the specific products they represented. The Brands that—because they were special—were purchased at a premium and produced quality profits.

Some of them have simply vanished; ceased to exist in the pandemonium of mergers, acquisitions and takeovers. They were altered and adapted and added to; in some cases, their logotypes were unnecessarily changed; they were made to represent products and services alien to their origins. There's only so much the brain and the heart can withstand before they proceed to suspect, reject and, ultimately, forget.

Some Brands were stretched beyond belief. Here's how I was made to feel about a favorite airline: I love you because you fly airplanes to far away places. But now you tell me you also manage hotels, cruises and credit cards. And you sold the route to my favorite far away place. And your pilots went on strike. And you are cheaper than Cheap Airways. And all of a sudden you are no longer a Brand. You are a commodity. You are an upgradeable seat. You are a Mileage Program, at best. Lose your specialness and you've lost me.

Some have jeopardized their heritage. Here's how I felt about my choice of a car company: I love you because you make the best cars in the world. I'm loyal to your products because of consistency—of style, quality, price, service, etc. But now you tell me that distinctive shape has to go—times have changed! And they are front wheel drive. Or four wheel drive. And you are no longer just in cars—you make jet engines and food processors as well. And you are no longer a Brand. You are a conglomerate.

Well, you are too big for my garage, now.

And some have changed their stories: I love you because you make me feel good when you talk to me. You are interesting; you are warm; you are honest; you are exciting. You are consistent; cohesive; trustworthy. But now you tell me you are also new and state-of-the-art and high tech. And you tell me you are better than A, B, C and D. And you have less of what you had before but offer more than you did before. And you are no longer available in the old pack I loved so much but look at this new one with the bright new colors and the Brand new logo. And you have introduced new varieties—in fact, if I like you, why shouldn't I like all your brothers and sisters and cousins and relatives? Trouble is, I don't *recognize* you anymore. You have changed so much, you have let me down.

If you look back on the world you grew up in, you will find yourself staring at a graveyard of wonderful Brands you grew up with and wish were still here. They were mismanaged into oblivion. Conversely, the star on the hood; the blue box with the jewel inside; the Tiger; the bunny that never gets tired; the little dough-boy and the jolly green giant; the contour bottle and the puppy pulling the little girls' bathing suit are still with us.

Brands exist to make our decision-making easier. To orient us. Which means they must both evolve and be themselves. My message is to all of you who shape and manage and breathe life into a Brand every day is very simple: *cherish* that Brand, *protect* that Brand, *add value* to that Brand, *perpetuate* that Brand.

By all means embrace change—change is the fuel of life. Make our new and distinctive look, your compelling and distinctive campaign—rooted in your origins but aimed at your future—represent positive change.

Please provide a better product and a better service—that will enhance your Brand's image. Please improve life—that will generate loyalty, if such a notion is still a realistic one to entertain. Above all, *be true* to that Brand.

And the best way to do that is to maintain uninterrupted dialogue with the consumer—listen to her, talk to her, carefully monitor her perceptions and feelings towards your Brand.

Because the future *is not* a commodity.

*"Understanding what makes Consumers tick is the most valuable contribution we can make to a Client's business."*

*"Never go backwards: Every new step is a benchmark.*
*I believe forward is the only direction—growth:*
*—creates jobs, wealth and confidence;*
*—eliminates fear, doubt and uncertainty;*
*—focuses on ideas, clients, prospects;*
*—puts our future in our hands;*
*—allows us to invest in our people/product."*

# The Difference Between
# Men And Boys Is The Size
# Of Their Brands

In 1987, I took a break from designing and executing ads and commercials and moved to California to be one of the marketing advisors at Columbia Pictures.

What did I learn in Hollywood?

Importantly, I learned that—with some exception—there are no established Brands in the motion picture industry. It is—and will regrettably continue to be—a hit-and-run business.

In other words, you front-load on the marketability of the product; cut the spend while you wait for audience response; and then survive on playability and word-of-mouth.

Additional investment may be required, but only if the trade—the exhibitors—insist on it.

I found myself establishing a parallel between the movie business and the toy business. Success is unpredictable and often short-lived. Advertising must be immediately effective. Seasonality and short lifecycles often make investment in advertising an act of faith. Advertising budgets can be canceled or increased at short notice.

And—with one or two admirable exceptions—there are no established Brands in the toy business either.

How do I define an established Brand? I believe that the primary job of a Brand is to make the buying decision easier and more satisfying to a customer.

In exchange for this clarity, the Brand is rewarded three-fold by the customer. First, with *sales*. Second, with *loyalty*. And third, with *increased margins*.

In a world of extraordinary choices within product categories, and fewer discriminating properties differentiating these choices, I believe those qualities which a Brand stands for (i.e. its Brand equity) are the heart and soul of it profitability. They are also the core of potential for further profitability through line extensions.

We all know the task of creating, evolving, and managing the equity of Brands has never been more difficult.

Retail distribution is increasingly more powerful and sophisticated. Technological advantage is harder to maintain. The cost of new product is extremely high. Product line extensions have proliferated beyond the grasp of consumers. As a result, consumer segmentation and the subsequent share battles, have intensified.

In our minds, it is the ability to constantly focus and refresh the equity for which a Brand stands that gives it its power over time.

This means making the commonplace *uncommonly special*; the usual *unusually interesting*; the ordinary extraordinarily *relevant*; and the innovative *believably unique*.

To successfully do so over time enhances a Brand's authority in its category. I believe Brand authority, that is, what a consumer believes a Brand is good at—is also what makes it so difficult for a new entry to penetrate the category.

In political terms, it is the authority of the incumbent. And unseating the incumbent is a rare event. Which is why it makes so much sense economically that established Brands are extending products across categories.

Furthermore, I believe that amongst Brands in technologically dependent categories Brand authority is an even more fragile entity because the consumer is learning he can trust the technology instead of the Brand.

Finally, assuming we have a Brand; assuming our Brand has an equity, an authority, a culture all its own—replicating its success from country to country requires experience and a system to control the translation of headquarters' objectives into effective local advertising.

There are the differing strategic needs of different companies, each using advertising to solve problems or exploit opportunities that sometimes are similar across markets. Understanding the value of multicultural advertising is appreciating the extent to which common solutions to multi-country business problems are possible. More brain power can be concentrated and applied against a consolidated and larger opportunity.

This is in many ways the opportunity—and the risk—of a Europe without borders. The idea is not to march in first with a multi-country solution—whether it be advertising or product development—without first knowing whether the opportunity or problem is in fact a multicultural one to begin with.

Let's look at this from the point of view of toys. One can take the same either/or approach as we did with global advertising.

Let's start with the negative view. Of course you can't do multicultural toy advertising in Europe. Even if one conceded that pan-European advertising would work for some adult products, it would not for children's products.

— Isn't it in the raising of children that we are most different as cultures? Isn't it in the intimate relationship between parents and children that values are instilled that in fact define different cultures?

— And the regulations on toy advertising differ so significantly market to market that too much of a hindrance is placed on creativity to be able to devise any single campaign.

So one would have to conclude, wouldn't one, that the best and only path is a single country ad campaign which understands the special attitudes of parents and children in that culture and which builds advertising addressing the distinct regulatory problems in that market.

Now, the so-called opposing point of view. Let's look at what is becoming similar among parents and children from one country to another and how that might lead to advertising.

— For one thing, we know that there are generation changes in every country. Today's parents are not like yesterday's, and no group of adults has been so like each other across countries. Many values, particularly those affecting consumer behavior, that are being imparted by this new generation of parents to his or her child in Italy are not as different today as those being taught to a child in Holland.

— Apart from the parents, let's look at the world the children are growing up in. They are watching more television and computers than in the past, an increasing amount of it programming that children in other countries are watching as well. Many of the Brand names or characters they are increasingly in contact with are those also familiar to children in other countries.

— It is a reasonable conclusion, backed up by observation in the toy market, that cultural differentiation of values and preferences develops gradually towards maturity. Experience shows that children react emotionally very spontaneously without influence of specific cultural norms.

Whereas adults react differently to say, chromium plated cars or status symbol personal accessories with large logos, children react to things that are bright, pretty cute etc. For example, little girls around the world seem to love bright pink as a color, whereas adults in some countries associate pink with 'low class' or poor taste.

For these reasons much of the advertising directed at children has more opportunity to be multicultural than has advertising to adults with their more complex culturally-dependent attitudes.

So enough commonality exists to create advertising. More importantly, enough commonality exists to create Brands—I mean Brands that have similar meanings across different countries.

I am in favor of global advertising, when it can legitimately be done. And the reason has nothing to do with it as advertising. It is not just an advertising issue. It is a business-building issue. If there are changes in a country that allow for consideration of a shared advertising approach, that means there is a discovery of a bigger business opportunity, one that didn't exist the day before under old parameters and borders.

I am a supporter of global advertising and of global Brands.

It's the power of a Brand to signify values that go deeper that a single sales transaction for a product.

Brand advertising can be created that has both national and global resonance at the same time. People like being part of something bigger and more scope, especially when it's in search of something that's the real thing.

But some critics of global advertising say that, yes, it may work for a product where imagery is important, but not in difficult pre-sensitive or product-benefit-explanation situations. That criticism, like many, is an oversimplification. But it is a point that does have great relevance to the toy industry.

Advertising imagery is not minor when one considers the visual world that children are accustomed to. It is very, very sophisticated, as advanced as cartoons and electronic games.

Add to this an even increasingly single borderless market in Europe that will continue to be one of many languages. Visual elements will be needed more to communicate in all types of categories for all ages. The fact that children have their own visual language such as cartoons and electronic games will be a big plus in communicating to them no matter where they are living.

And this is the key. The point is not that you are advertising in France or Italy or using one campaign or two, but that you understand the mind of the child you are reaching. To that child, your marketing plan doesn't matter. What matters is what he or she sees, and whether it's relevant.

Once you have established a Brand, not only consumers will recognize you and respect you, the competition will do the same. And, as they say, imitation is sincerest form of flattery.

The issue is to communicate with one Brand, one set of values, which can be applied to different products, different audiences, different markets.

In my view, a Brand must be managed simultaneously from three perspectives:

— what it has historically stood for;

— what we need from it today;

— what we expect from it tomorrow.

Neglecting the first denies leverage. Neglecting the second denies reality. Neglecting the third denies the future.

As I said at the beginning, it's not the size of your toys—it's the size of your Brands.

*"Create Work That Wins"*

# Work *That* Works
# Work *That* Wins

Dictionaries define Creativity as "the capability of inventing or producing original or imaginative work." Clearly, this is a broad definition and refers, equally to a host of creative manifestations, ranging from the fine arts to architectural engineering to product design.

The idea behind "Work *That* Works, Work *That* Wins" is that we are in a business where if the commercials, the ad pieces that we develop for digital, for the Internet, don't actually sell products—we don't have a job. Hence, Work *That* Works.

But a lot of work that works is not particularly brilliant. It's not particularly well designed. So, that is where the second half of this equation comes from—Work *That* Wins.

We all know that if your work wins something at a Festival, not only it is *effective* but it is also hopefully *brilliant* or has some degree of brilliance.

Creativity is a broad realm, and applies to all kinds of human endeavor. Creativity and Marketing Communications, however, must be more precisely defined. Since the objective of Marketing Communications is to impact diverse audiences, of diverse origins, social strata and age groups, and at diverse stages of development; Creativity must be *applied* with:

a) tangible and measurable results expectations. (You are not creating to please yourself, you are not creating for an audience that just wants to praise your work. You are creating to achieve something) and,

b) a keen sense of lifestyle and cultural currency. (It should not be created in a vacuum. It should be part of the world we live in.)

In addition, therefore, to being inventive, original and imaginative, *Applied Creativity* must also be target-sensitive, response-generating, and results-oriented. In other words, it must stand out in the clutter of the competitive landscape, and it must touch Consumers in a relevant, demand-creating manner.

We need to know who we are talking to—target sensitive. There was a time when we wrote ads, put them in a magazine, and that was it. Hopefully people bought the magazine, opened the magazine and read our ad.

Today, you know almost immediately if somebody was impacted by your idea, by your commercial, with a click.

The whole idea behind Work *That* Works, Work *That* Wins was to design a proprietary, a way of articulating our vision of effective advertising.

Effective advertising, per se, expresses a performance dimension but fails to convey the dimensions of creativity, originality, impact and brand-building capability that we must demand of all our ideas. Clients like to hear it because it says, accountable; Creatives don't like to hear it because it says trodden territory, been there, done that.

Award winning advertising doesn't do it either precisely because it lacks the accountability factor. Most client dismiss it as a "creative thing."

And yet Clients and Agency people alike would agree that nothing beats a superior end product. One that outperforms competition. One that is talked about. One that stands out. One that commands premium pricing. One that earns peer recognition.

But how do you get a Work *That* Works, Work *That* Wins?

First, we must make sure that the Consumer is accurately and legitimately represented in the work. Without valid Consumer information and keen Consumer insights we are back to "let's look at the creative and then write the strategy."

Then, we must apply brains. In a parity world, where only the top two or three Brands will survive, our strategies must provide an edge. They must leave competition behind and lead the way to inspired, original creativity.

Last but not least—and probably the most controversial one—we must fight decades of a non-fighting spirit in our own industry.

The words are all there: do not be denied; refuse to lose.

There are times when we don't fight because there's not enough time to do better.

There are times when we don't fight because it's good enough as it is.

There are times when we don't fight because that's just the way this Client is.

There are times when we don't fight because it could disturb the relationship.

There are times when we don't fight because sure there's a cheaper photographer that can get a similar result.

There are times when we don't fight because that's just the Creative Director being precious.

Not to mention the times when we drop a riskier, more daring idea so as not to pick a fight.

My formula is:

Work *That* Works means effectiveness in the marketplace; ideas that help effect sales; accountable performance that can be legitimately attributed to our contribution.

The second set of W's stands for Work *That* Wins, which means industry recognition in the form of awards, press coverage, reputations and—not to be forgotten—being perceived as a great agency to work for.

If we truly expect—as a craft and as an industry—to earn the respect of our Clients, to become their most valuable marketing partners, then we are going to need a generous and balanced measure of brains and brawn (solid and well developed muscles; muscular strength).

Brains with which to conceive, originate and express.

Brawn with which to dare, to push, to insist and never give up.

Brains for the flight, brawn for the fight.

Brains plus brawn will generate Work *That* Works, Work *That* Wins. When we use our brains, it shows in the quality of our ideas. That when we exercise brawn, we add edge to what we create, to what we sell, and to how we express it.

*"Cherish, Respect, Nurture and Protect Ideas."*

*"Measuring Up—The Creative Tool"*

How do we stimulate creativity among ourselves?

How do you do that when you are with a partner or just by yourself trying to come up with something?

How do you evaluate what you created?

Measuring up was developed to be a practical framework in the pursuit of Creativity. I didn't do this by myself, I had a lot of help, but it is my baby in many ways, because I have been working on it for a long time, and using it not only for McCann, for myself, but with diverse groups around the world. It has been translated in several languages.

While it primarily seeks to stimulate and accelerate Creativity, it can also be used to evaluate it from *Originality/Inventiveness* point of view.

### 1. Create, Not Replicate:

How many times have you seen an idea on television, on the Internet, or somewhere else, that looks familiar, that sounds like something you have seen before.

So, the first rule is *create*, in other words, try to be as original as you can from the get go. Do not replicate other ideas.

### 2. See The World Through Fresh Eyes:

This is particular easier if you are younger, or somebody who has been doing this for a long time. People tend to approach things the same way, every time out of the box. And all you need to do is to try on fresh eyes everyday. Walk away from where you have been from your normal approach would be, and try to see it with fresh eyes.

*3. Stand In A Different Place And Describe What You See:*

It is fascinating when you are sitting somewhere thinking about something you have been putting hours into it, and you stay in a certain territory. But if you physically walk down the room, turn back and look at it again. Or look at it from a different angle. Or focus on a different word or element of design, you will see that it can be done differently. And that is a trigger for originality. If you are able to describe what you see having moved yourself to a different place, physically or mentally, it is another great way to design fresh thinking.

*4. Speak With An Original Voice:*

Original voice, different graphics, choice of words, or actual voice. But the key is *originality.*

A lot of what we see today, sounds like something else; feels like something else. I will give you an example: most car commercials look like other car commercials. Occasionally, if you remove the Brand from the back end of the commercial, we don't actually know which car they are trying to sell you. We are not the only one responsible, for it. The Clients are responsible for it too. They all want the same shots and you end up with a commercial made of clichés.

Speaking with an original voice, means we sometimes must go against the grain. That isn't what is expected.

*5. Connect What Others Have Not Seen As A Connection:*

It is very common for Clients that seek the same type of idea for a certain amount of time, then they say they need something new. The problem is that the Consumer is not quite as tired of it as the Client is. And if you can look at it differently standing in a different place, looking with fresh eyes, and doing it again, it has a value—because it is already established.

### 6. Create Messages That Consumers Wish To Consume:

It is not good to have a wonderful message if the Consumer is not particularly interested, or attracted to it. What do people get out of the message. That's the key.

### 7. Dramatize A Penetrating Truth About Our Clients Brands:

Connect to something that matters.

### 8. Tell The Truth So Well That The Customer Is Converted:

The motivating thing about making a purchase is that there is something in the product, or about the product or in the Brand that speaks to you. If you can find out what that is, call it the truth about that and dramatize it—and that's the idea. Tell the truth so well that the people can be converted.

There is another notion—people can be convinced, people can be persuaded, all of those things are temporary and they can be left on the side of the road. But when people are converted—that's a whole other deal. That means I have adopted that, that's what I like. That's what I am going to do. That's very difficult these days. But the whole concept of Brand loyalty comes from the idea of conversion.

Measuring up is simplicity itself: It's what stimulates and helps evaluate creativity: be exclusively concerned with *Innovation, Freshness, Inventiveness and Originality,* characteristics which are inherently essential to the creative process. In other words, they are the principles of *Uniqueness.*

We may not achieve it every time out of the box. And it is very hard to achieve it. But the creative side of the business is the pursuit of the *uniqueness.* The pursuit of something unheard of, untold before, undesigned in the way that you design it. Even if it is a little fragment of novelty to it, that's what you are looking for.

By the way, if that works, and if it is done properly, that wins. Be exclusively concerned with *Connection, Interaction, Persuasion and Conversion,* characteristics which are inherently essential to the selling process. In other words, they are the principles of *Effectiveness.*

*Measuring up:* A tool that questions your sense of originality, challenges your quality standards, maximizes your imagination and helps produce: *Effective Creativity*—creativity that works, *Applied Creativity.*

"I don't care if anybody says, but if the Client is paying you to design something, to promote his Brand or product; he is expecting *effectiveness, creativity, originality and uniqueness.*"

But how do you judge Effective Creativity?

These are questions designed to make sure you are in the presence of *Real Ideas*, not mere *Executional Solutions.* These can be helpful in creating *common evaluation language* among the various disciplines involved in the project.

If you live in an ad Agency, the person from the media department has his own ideas of what should be done; the person in the account management group, has his own ideas on what should be done and of course the Client when you finally meet with him has his own ideas.

And if you don't have a *common language* between them it is almost impossible to come to an agreement as to what is the best idea for the Brand.

These questions are designed to create *common language* between the various constituencies.

*"Effective Creativity"*

I believe in compelling Ideas that build Brands. Ideas that understand the complex relationships between Consumers and their preferred Brands. That add facets and dimensions and intensity to those relationships, making them richer, stronger and longer lasting. And I believe there are two crucial triggers you must pull if trying to develop effective, highly creative advertising:

— *substance* in the strategy and

— *brilliance* in the execution.

Our definition of effective communication, therefore, reads like this:

*Compelling advertising, that builds or reinforces a bond between Consumers and Brands, with something substantial to tell, told brilliantly.*

I believe in Function first, Form second. Idea first, Execution second. Function enhanced by Form. Idea improved by Execution. Get the right balance between them and you've got powerful communication. Add consistency and you may even end up with a big idea that works over time and over borders.

Too many ads provide you with answers to questions you haven't asked. How do you make sure you are being relevant to people?

What seems to work for me is what I call the interrogation process.

First, interrogate the product. What is it about a product that makes it the answer to a legitimate question? What's in a product that makes it a better answer than others? Does the product define its category or is it one of many within it? Does it have a culture? A following? What does it do best?

Second, interrogate the maker. The inventor, the owner, the engineer, the chemist, the designer, the quality controller, the dealer, the bottler, the packer, you name it. These people know things that don't show up in strategy documents. They know things they don't know are important.

And third, interrogate the user. People don't know what they don't know. People know how they feel. People know what they think. Registering behavior is a science; projecting behavior is an art form. To remain relevant, a Brand or product must constantly take risks. Creativity is a risky business.

In essence, we try to get people to think before they act. To ensure direction before the creative process begins. To provide insights to help guide the creative process.

The way I see it, there's no relevance, no creative brilliance without strategic substance.

Effective advertising is not about what we say, it's about what people understand. It's about eliciting and obtaining a response. Heavy, qualified traffic, on a two-way street. Telephones and cash registers ringing. Brands and products becoming a part of people's lives as a result of compelling, persuasive communication.

Achieving relevance is a balancing act. It helps to have a good and useful product to start with. But, in the end, its success will depend upon it. Not rational versus emotional, but the rational emotional reasons for preference and, with any luck, long-term loyalty.

In the past, Brand builders everywhere became acutely aware of the power of emotional bonding in attracting and retaining consumers. We all learned which emotional buttons to push to make our Brands and products special to people.

In the meantime, pressures from the trade, from intensified competition, from price wars, from private labels—have somewhat reduced, at least temporarily, the efficacy of emotional bonding strategies.

Rational relevance becomes as important as, or more, in some cases than emotional relevance.

Understanding and reflecting the reality surrounding Consumers is key to achieving relevance. Education, aspirations, the social setting, the media scene, the government—all of these factors impact Consumers and the risk of ignoring them is total irrelevance.

Keep it simple and helpful to the brain; make it warm and friendly to the heart; try to strike the right balance between the two—and it just might work.

As creative professionals, whether we operate in Dublin or Durban, in Minneapolis or Manila, in Sidney or Santiago, our job is not done until we have created energy, until we have moved men and women into stores and products into homes, until we've made sales.

Last but not least—brilliance.

Brilliance sometimes comes from being able to zig when everyone else is zagging. Calm down when others hurry up. Dialogue when others sing and dance.

The people we cultivate and learn to trust are the innovators who help us innovate. These men and women are a creative person's strategic alliances. They are there to complement and supplement the insights, the accuracy, the intimacy with a Client's problem that only the creative person has.

A. Can The Idea Be Put Into Words?

Put your idea into words that anybody can understand. It isn't about borrowing bits and pieces from other places and thinking that is enough to explain an idea. It is really a defense weapon against derivative thinking. If the presenter cannot convince you with words, you are probably in the presence of an executional-driven concept. This does not mean it is a bad approach or irrelevant to the problem you are trying to solve. It means it is borrowing some of its persuasion from other existing sources.

### B. Is The Brand/Product Central?

Very important. A lot of we hear today and we see today is just "stuff"—brought to you by so and so. A lot of "stuff"—interesting graphics, interesting sounds etc. And then when you least expect, a Brand comes up at the end of that and says, by the way, "we are here." That is not *Central*!

Or the case may be, make my product central. This one is aimed at avoiding advertising purely as an art form, with no consequence to the product or Brand being advertised. Consumers expect advertising to help them make decisions, rationally or emotionally or both. They expect clarity.

### C. What Is The Breakthrough Consumer Insight?

Is there one? If there isn't one, are you willing to come up with one—the penetrating idea mentioned before?

### D. Is It Original And Relevant?

Not everything will be original, but one thing is for sure, everything needs to be relevant, if not, it won't work.

Be original but relevant is both a reminder to you—as the importance of originality, innovation, creativity—and to the creative people—

as the importance of purpose in advertising. The purpose is to deliver a memorable message to Consumers, not just to flash exciting images before their eyes.

E. Is It An Idea or Just An Execution?

Anything that is totally reliant on executional values, for example graphics or sounds etc, is lacking in an idea as the center.

The creative DNA is Ideas, not Executions.

F. Can It Be Extended Across Platforms?

And of course in order to be effective it has to be extended across platforms. These days you cannot come up with something that only works for example in YouTube. It will have to work in all kinds of other media. Therefore the big test for an idea is how do you translate that into the proper language for each of the new media or even the traditional media that you are working with.

Connect me with my Consumer is yet again a defense mechanism against creative solutions that ignore or alienate your target Consumer in favor of a trendy but possibly irrelevant executional format. You know what I mean: banks that look like soft-drinks; beers that behave like champagne etc.

Most of the time, advertising is effective because you can see yourself in it. You look at it and you say: that could be me. This is advertising created to connect, not to impress. Consumers respond to it because it is relevant to the way they live, the way they wish to live, or even the way they don't want to live.

Too much of what is deemed to be highly creative advertising is often too topical, too narrow or too short-lived to become a real property for a Brand. If you are looking for a campaign Idea that will work over time and over borders; across all media as well as below and above the line—then you want size and extensibility.

I urge Clients to encourage, nurture, cherish and support creativity from their agencies. I urge them to give them clear briefs and intellectual freedom. I urge them to be respectful of the creative process, which can be arduous and painful.

But I also urge Clients to help their creative people avoid the ephemeral, the superficial and the irrelevant—the executional trappings that so many times mask the absence of a solid idea.

This is all important because when you go to the Client and you put this in front of him before you present the idea, now you have something to talk about, now you have questions to be answered, now you have a common language.

But if you don't have common language, it is going to be a very long discussion, probably not leading to a great result.

Advertising, as we know it, isn't just going to disappear off the face of the earth. It will transform itself, something borrowed, something new, until it becomes what it will be next. But—to repeat the cliché—newspapers weren't erased by radio, radio wasn't turned off by television, and television won't be deleted by Online communications. Everything gets repositioned and continues to play one role or another.

Creatively, some of us have been busy sharpening our interactive skills as interactivity will play a key role in involving Consumers. Embellished, state-of-the-art, special effects laden one-way communication will be less intriguing than information that must be decoded before it is consumed. Unadorned but challenging will do better than beautiful but easy.

G. Does It Have *Scope*?

*Is It True To The Brand's DNA?*

Ideas must cross borders and disciplines. Consumers are more universal in their motivations and, in fact, understand more languages that the experts give them credit for.

I refer, of course, to the tried and true and ever so persuasive languages of effective advertising. There are many of them, but the ones I would like to illustrate are:

— *Emotion*

— *Identification*

— *Music*

— *Demonstration*

— *Simplicity*

— *Humor*

— *Consistency*

Let's start with the most controversial one: *emotion.*

The English and the Australians wouldn't touch it; the Japanese use it but we wouldn't understand it; Latins are known for it but don't use it much; and the Americans couldn't live without it.

Sometimes advertising is effective because you can see yourself in it. You look at it and you say: that could be me. This is advertising created to connect, not to impress. Consumers respond to it because it is relevant to the way they live.

Many creative people believe *music* is primarily the idiom of youth—that's why soft-drinks, blue jeans and other youth-driven products use it so much. Truth is, music goes much beyond age, culture, gender, politics—it brings people together in a most powerful manner.

If your product has something tangible, something visible to offer, don't just say it, *show it.*

Less is more. Why complicate? Many advertising propositions lose their way because of creative complexity. Complications of argument, plot or execution which make them difficult to follow. And, therefore difficult to like. Just as Brands *simplify* Consumer decisions, simple advertising succeeds because Consumers appreciate *clarity* above all else. But perhaps the most delicate, most vulnerable, most challenging advertising idiom of all is *humor.*

Humor varies from person to person, let alone culture to culture. Because people's reactions to humor can range from disinterest to amusement; from uncontrollable laughter to absolute indignation.

While all of the above weapons—emotion, identification, music, simplicity and humor—can improve the effectiveness of your advertising, none will hit the target with more tangible, longer-lasting results than *consistency.*

Unfortunately, no Festival, no Award Show I know of gives out a prize for *consistency.* Consumers give out prizes for *consistency:* they buy the product; they become loyal to the Brand; they pay a premium to get the Brand they perceive to be the best.

*Consistency* is key when you launch a Brand.

*Consistency* is key when you revitalize a Brand.

*Consistency* is key when you want a Brand to live happily ever after.

Compelling advertising, that builds or reinforces a bond between Consumers and Brands, with something substantial to tell, told brilliantly.

This is effective advertising.

*"Choice isnt about having choice, it is about believing there is a choice."*

*"Start with a focused idea: it refreshes me,*
*satisfies me, and connects me—*
*it makes everything better for me.*
*Nothing else makes me*
*feel so right."*

# Inventiveness:
# The Brazilian Advantage

Most Brazilians of my generation grew up reading Monteiro Lobato, later Jorge Amado, later Guimarães Rosa, to mention but three of the most imaginative authors in world literature. This same streak of inventiveness and creativity pervades all forms of artistic expression in the Brazilian culture, from Music to Sculpture to Painting to Architecture—to the point where Brazilians have come to take it for granted.

And the Brazilian Popular Culture is just as full of powerful examples of the national love of inventiveness: the country has transformed the Portuguese language; has redefined football; has developed its own music, again and again; has shot movies and manufactured airplanes; has blended the races like no other culture; has elevated soap operas to nearly an art form.

It has mistakenly elected leaders and adopted economic models because they claimed to be different and innovative. It continues to have a blind faith in things and people because they are "different". Brazilians love to be on the edge of things; to live "in the zone"; to incur that margin of error that can lead to either total disaster or absolute greatness. "Eight or eighty", Brazilians are fond of saying.

This all-or-nothing, big-risk-big-reward mindset lives and thrives in Brazilian creative departments, as well. It is never enough to do just what the Client asked for; it is never enough simply to move products off shelves; the ideas must be talked about. They must become part of the popular culture. They must be current and memorable and—above all—award-winning.

In this regard, Brazilian advertising creativity is not dissimilar from Brazilian creativity in other manifestations such as auto racing, fashion, modeling, entertainment and sports. The country seems to suffer from an almost obsessive need to stand out and be celebrated; to be compensated, through international recognition, for being the stage for so many unresolved social and economic woes.

And an ad—for a Brazilian adman—is an opportunity to shine, never to be wasted. This explains why Brazilian advertising creativity is among the most acclaimed in the international creative community, winning a comparatively disproportionate share of top awards in Cannes, London, New York and throughout Latin America. Brazil is an established member of a very exclusive club of global winners. This makes it easy to get carried away, sometimes: to create ideas for awards shows, not to sell products; to craft catch phrases and arresting visuals without a clear strategy; to consider the creative competition more important than persuading consumers to buy products and be loyal to Brands.

Creativity and inventiveness are the Brazilian antidotes to an ever-changing economic and political environment; to consumer disinterest and disillusion; to old formulas that rely on message repetition rather than retention. When a Brazilian ad is on, it is almost invariably as captivating, or more, than the programming it is inserted into. And it helps keep the economy churning.

This is no small achievement for a bunch of creative people whose challenge is to fill blank sheets of paper with ideas. Every day.

Lightning Source UK Ltd.
Milton Keynes UK
UKHW011837310720
367514UK00004B/5/J